The Meaning of the War
Henri Bergson

Contents

THE MEANING OF THE WAR 7
INTRODUCTION 7
LIFE AND MATTER AT WAR 9
THE FORCE WHICH WASTES 18
AND THAT WHICH DOES NOT WASTE 18

THE MEANING OF THE WAR

BY

Henri Bergson

THE MEANING OF THE WAR
LIFE & MATTER IN CONFLICT
BY HENRI BERGSON
WITH AN INTRODUCTION BY H. WILDON CARR

INTRODUCTION

THIS little volume contains the discourse delivered by M. Bergson as President of the *Academie des Sciences Morales et Politiques* at its annual public meeting on December 12, 1914. It is the address which preceded the announcement of the prizes and awards bestowed by the Academy. It is now issued in book form with the consent of the author, and his full appreciation of the object, to give it the widest circulation. Although it is brief, it is a message addressed directly to the heart of our people in the crisis of war. To it is added a short article on the same theme, contributed to the *Bulletin des Armees de la Republique*, November 4, 1914.

It has been said that war, with all its terrible evils, is the occasion of at least one good which humanity values as above price: it inspires great poetry. On the other hand, it seems to crush philosophy. Many may think that in this message it is poetry to which M. Bergson is giving expression. It is, however, from the depth of his philosophy that the inspiration is drawn. The full significance of the doctrines he has been teaching, and their whole moral and political bearing, are brought into clear light, focussed, as it were, on the actual present struggle. Yet is there no word that breathes hatred to any person or to any race. It is by the triumph of a spiritual principle that philosophy may hope to free humanity from the oppression of a materialist doctrine.

The opposing principle has had, and still has, philosophers to defend it, and they belong to no particular nation or race. One of its most brilliant and influential exponents was a Frenchman, the diplomatist, Comte Joseph Arthur de Gobineau (1816-1882). A brief word on this remarkable man may help the reader to understand the mention of his name on page 30. His *Essai sur l'inegalite des races humaines* (1855) was the first of a series of writings to affirm, on ethnological grounds, the superiority of the Aryan race, and its right and destiny by reason of that superiority to rule all other races as bondsmen. He was the friend of Wagner, and also of Nietzsche. Madame Foerster-Nietzsche in her biography of her brother has spoken of the almost reverent regard which he entertained for Gobineau, and it may be that from him Nietzsche derived the idea which he developed into his doctrine of the non-morality of the superman.

Were the discourse of M. Bergson no more than the utterance of a philosopher stirred by deep patriotic feeling to uphold his country's cause and denounce his country's foes, then, however eloquent its appeal, it would have no significance or value beyond its present power to inspire courage in the hearts of his comrades. And it would not differ from equally earnest appeals which other philosophers have addressed to the world on behalf of their fellow-countrymen. It has a much deeper meaning. It is no mere indictment of modern Germany's rulers or people. It goes to the very heart of the problem of the future of humanity. Shall the splendid material progress which has marked the scientific achievement of the last century be the forging of a sword to destroy the freedom which life has won with it from matter?

As these words are written the conflict is raging, and the decision seems still far off. Death is striking down the young in all the nations, and among them many on whom our highest hopes were founded. "But whatever be the price of victory," so writes M. Bergson to me, "it will not have been too dearly bought if humanity is finally delivered from the nightmare which weighs on it."

H. WILDON CARR
LONDON, *May 1915*

LIFE AND MATTER AT WAR

"Comprendre et ne pas s'indigner": this has been said to be the last word of philosophy. I believe none of it; and, had I to choose, I should much prefer, when in presence of crime, to give my indignation rein and not to understand. Happily, the choice has not to be made. On the contrary, there are forms of anger which, by a thorough comprehension of their objects, derive the force to sustain and renew their vigour. Our anger is of that kind. We have only to detach the inner meaning of this war, and our horror for those who made it will be increased. Moreover, nothing is easier. A little history, and a little philosophy, will suffice.

For a long period Germany devoted herself to poetry, to art, to metaphysic. She was made, so she said, for thought and imagination; "she had no feeling for the reality of things." It is true that her administration had defects, that she was divided into rival states, that anarchy at certain times seemed beyond remedy. Nevertheless, an attentive study would have revealed, beneath this disorder, the normal process of life, which is always too rank at the first and later on prunes away its excess, makes its choice and adopts a lasting form. From her municipal activity there would have issued at length a good administration which would have assured order without suppressing liberty. From the closer union of the confederated states that unity in diversity, which is the distinguishing mark of organized beings, would have arisen. But time was needed for that, as it always is needed by life, in order that its possibilities may be realized.

Now, while Germany was thus working out the task of her organic self-development there was within her, or rather by her side, a people with whom every process tended to take a mechanical form. Artificiality marked the creation of Prussia; for she was formed by clumsily sewing together, edge to edge, provinces either acquired or conquered. Her administration was mechanical; it did its work with the regularity of a well-appointed machine. Not less mechanical--extreme both in precision and in power--was the army, on which the attention of the Hohenzollerns was concentrated. Whether it was that the people had been drilled for centuries to mechanical obedience; or that an elemental instinct for conquest and plunder, absorbing to itself the life of the nation, had simplified its aims and reduced them to materialism; or that the Prussian character was originally so made--it is certain that the idea of Prussia always evoked a vision of rudeness, of rigidity, of automatism, as if everything within her went by clockwork, from the gesture of her kings to the step of her soldiers.

A day came when Germany had to choose between a rigid and ready-made system of unification, mechanically superposed from without, and the unity which comes from within by a natural effort of life. At the same time the choice was offered her between an administrative mechanism, into which she would merely have to fit herself--a complete order, doubtless, but poverty-stricken, like everything else that is artificial--and that richer and more flexible order which the wills of men, when freely associated, evolve of themselves. How would she choose?

There was a man on the spot in whom the methods of Prussia were incarnate--a genius, I admit, but an evil genius; for he was devoid of scruple, devoid of faith, devoid of pity, and devoid of soul. He had just removed the only obstacle which could spoil his plan; he had got rid of Austria. He said to himself: "We are going to make Germany take over, along with Prussian centralization and discipline, all our ambitions and all our appetites. If she hesitates, if the confederate peoples do not arrive of their own accord at this common resolution, I know how to compel them; I will cause a breath of hatred to pass over them, all alike. I will launch them against a common enemy, an enemy we have hood-winked and waylaid, and whom we shall try to catch unarmed. Then when the hour of triumph shall sound, I will rise up; from Germany, in her intoxication, I will snatch a covenant, which, like that of Faust with Mephistopheles, she has signed with her blood, and by which she also, like Faust, has traded her soul away for the good things of earth."

He did as he had said. The covenant was made. But, to ensure that it would never be broken, Germany must be made to feel, for ever and ever, the necessity of the armour in which she was imprisoned. Bismarck took his measures accordingly. Among the confidences which fell from his lips and were gathered up by his intimates is this revealing word: "We took nothing from Austria after Sadowa because we wanted to be able one day to be reconciled with her." So, then, in taking Alsace and a part of Lorraine, his idea was that no reconciliation with the French would be possible. He intended that the German people should believe itself in permanent danger of war, that the new Empire should remain armed to the teeth, and that Germany, instead of dissolving Prussian militarism into her own life, should reinforce it by militarizing herself.

She reinforced it; and day by day the machine grew in complexity and power. But in the process it yielded automatically a result very different from that which its constructors had foreseen. It is the story of the witch who, by a magic incantation, had won the consent of her broomstick to go to the river and fill her buckets; having no formula ready to check the work, she watched her cave fill with water until she was drowned.

The Prussian army had been organized, brought to perfection, tended with love by the Kings of Prussia, in order that it might serve their lust of conquest. To take possession of neighbours' territory was then the sole aim; territory was almost the whole of the national wealth. But with the nineteenth century there was a new departure. The idea peculiar to that century of diverting science to the satisfaction of men's material wants evoked a development of industry, and consequently of commerce, so extraordinary that the old conception of wealth was completely overthrown. Not more than fifty years were needed to bring about this transformation. On the morrow of the war of 1870 a nation expressly made for appropriating the good things of this world had no alternative but to become industrial and commercial. Not on that account, however, would she change the essential principle of her action. On the contrary, she had but to utilize her habits of discipline, method, tenacity, minute care, precise information--and, we may add, of impertinence and spying--to which she owed the growth of her military power. She would thus equip herself with industry and commerce not less formidable than her army, and able to march, on their part also, in military order.

From that time onwards these two were seen going forward together, advancing at an even pace and reciprocally supporting each other--industry, which had answered the appeal of the spirit of conquest, on one side; on the other, the army, in which that spirit was incarnate, with the navy, which had just been added to the forces of the army. Industry was free to develop in all directions; but, from the first, war was the end in view. In enormous factories, such as the world had never seen, tens of thousands of workmen toiled in casting great guns, while by their side, in workshops and laboratories, every invention which the disinterested genius of neighbouring peoples had been able to achieve was immediately captured, bent from its intended use, and converted into an engine of war. Reciprocally, the army and navy which owed their growth to the increasing wealth of the nation, repaid the debt by placing their services at the disposal of this wealth: they undertook to open roads for commerce and outlets for industry. But through this very combination the movement imposed on Prussia by her kings, and on Germany by Prussia, was bound to swerve from its course, whilst gathering speed and flinging itself forward. Sooner or later it was bound to escape from all control and become a plunge into the abyss.

For, even though the spirit of conquest knows no limit in itself, it must limit its ambitions as long as the question is simply that of seizing a neighbour's territory. To constitute their kingdom, kings of Prussia had been obliged to undertake a long series of wars. Whether the name of the spoiler be Frederick or William, not more than one or two provinces can be annexed at a time: to take more is to weaken oneself. But suppose that the same insatiable thirst for conquest enters into the new form of wealth--what follows? Boundless ambition, which till then had spread out the coming of its gains over indefinite time, since each one of them would be worth only a definite portion of space, will now leap all at once to an object boundless as itself. Rights will be set up on every point of the globe where raw material for industry, refitting stations for ships, concessions for capitalists, or outlets for production are seen to exist. In fact, the policy which had served Prussia so well passed at a bound from the most calculating prudence to the wildest temerity. Bismarck, whose common-sense put some restraint on the logic of his principles, was still averse to colonial enterprises; he said that all the affairs of the East were not worth the bones of one Pomeranian grenadier. But Germany, retaining Bismarck's former impulse, went straight on and rushed forward along the lines of least resistance to east and west: on the one side lay the route to the Orient, on the other the empire of the sea. But in so doing she virtually declared war on the nations which Bismarck had managed to keep allied or friendly. Her ambition looked forward to the domination of the world.

Moreover, there was no moral restraint which could keep this ambition under control. Intoxicated by victory, by the prestige which victory had given her, and of which her commerce, her industry, her science even, had reaped the benefit, Germany plunged into a material prosperity such as she had never known, such as she would never have dared to dream of. She told herself that if force had wrought this miracle, if force had given her riches and honour, it was because force had within it a hidden virtue, mysterious--nay, divine. Yes, brute force with its train of trickery and lies, when it comes with powers of attack sufficient for the conquest of the world, must needs be in direct line from heaven and a revelation of the will of God on earth. The people to whom this power of attack had come were the elect, a chosen race by whose side the others are races of bondmen. To such a race nothing is forbidden that may help in establishing its dominion. Let none speak to it of inviolable right! Right is what is written in a treaty; a treaty is what registers the will of a conqueror--that is, the direction of his force for the time being: force, then, and right are the same thing; and if force is pleased to take a new direction, the old right becomes ancient history and the treaty, which backed it with a solemn undertaking, no more than a scrap of paper. Thus Germany, struck with wonder in presence of her victories, of the brute force which had been their means, of the material prosperity which was the outcome, translated her amazement into an idea. And see how, at the call of this idea, a thousand thoughts, as if awaked from slumber, and shaking off the dust of libraries, came rushing in from every side--thoughts which Germany had suffered to sleep among her poets and philosophers, every one which could lend a seductive or striking form to a conviction already made! Henceforth German imperialism had a theory of its own. Taught in schools and universities, it easily moulded to itself a nation already broken-in to passive obedience and having no loftier ideal wherewith to oppose the official doctrine. Many persons have explained the aberrations of German policy as due to that theory. For my part, I see in it nothing more than a philosophy doomed to translate into ideas what was, in its essence, insatiable ambition and will perverted by pride. The doctrine is an effect rather than a cause; and should the day come when Germany, conscious of her moral humiliation, shall say, to excuse herself, that she had trusted herself too much to certain theories, that an error of judgment is not a crime, it will then be necessary to remind her that her philosophy was simply a translation into intellectual terms of her brutality, her appetites, and her vices. So, too, in most cases, doctrines are the means by which nations and individuals seek to explain what they are and what they do. Germany, having finally become a predatory nation, invokes Hegel as witness; just as a Germany enamoured of moral beauty would have declared herself faithful to Kant, just as a sentimental Germany would have found her tutelary genius in Jacobi or Schopenhauer. Had she leaned in any other direction and been unable to find at home the philosophy she needed, she would have procured it from abroad. Thus when she wished to convince herself that predestined races exist, she took from France, that she might hoist him into celebrity, a writer whom we have not read--Gobineau.

None the less is it true that perverse ambition, once erected into theory, feels more at ease in working itself out to the end; a part of the responsibility will then be thrown upon logic. If the German race is the elect, it will be the only race which has an unconditional right to live; the others will be tolerated races, and this toleration will be precisely what is called "the state of peace." Let war come; the annihilation of the enemy will be the end Germany has to pursue. She will not strike at combatants only; she will massacre women, children, old men; she will pillage and burn; the ideal will be to destroy towns, villages, the whole population. Such is the conclusion of the theory. Now we come to its aim and true principle.

As long as war was no more than a means to the settlement of a dispute between two nations, the conflict was localized to the two armies involved. More and more of useless violence was eliminated; innocent populations were kept outside the quarrel. Thus little by little a code of war was drawn up. From the first, however, the Prussian army, organized as it was for conquest, did not take kindly to this law. But from the time when Prussian militarism, now turned into German militarism, had become one with industrialism, it was the enemy's industry, his commerce, the sources of his wealth, his wealth itself, as well as his military power, which war must now make the end in view. His factories must be destroyed that his competition may be suppressed. Moreover, that he may be impoverished once and for all and the aggressor enriched, his towns must be put to ransom, pillaged, and burned. Above all must the war be short, not only in order that the economic life of Germany might not suffer too much, but further, and chiefly, because her military power lacked that consciousness of a right superior to force by which she could sustain and recuperate her energies. Her moral force, being only the pride which comes from material force, would be exposed to the same vicissitudes as this latter: in proportion as the one was being expended the other would be used up. Time for moral force to become used up must not be given. The machine must deliver its blow all at once. And this it could do by terrorizing the population, and so paralysing the nation. To achieve that end, no scruple must be suffered to embarrass the play of its wheels. Hence a system of atrocities prepared in advance--a system as sagaciously put together as the machine itself.

Such is the explanation of the spectacle before us. "Scientific barbarism," "systematic barbarism," are phrases we have heard. Yes, barbarism reinforced by the capture of civilization. Throughout the course of the history we have been following there is, as it were, the continuous clang of militarism and industrialism, of machinery and mechanism, of debased moral materialism.

Many years hence, when the reaction of the past shall have left only the grand outline in view, this perhaps is how a philosopher will speak of it. He will say that the idea, peculiar to the nineteenth century, of employing science in the satisfaction of our material wants had given a wholly unforeseen extension to the mechanical arts and had equipped man in less than fifty years with more tools than he had made during the thousands of years he had lived on the earth. Each new machine being for man a new organ--an artificial organ which merely prolongs the natural organs--his body became suddenly and prodigiously increased in size, without his soul being able at the same time to dilate to the dimensions of his new body. From this disproportion there issued the problems, moral, social, international, which most of the nations endeavoured to solve by filling up the soulless void in the body politic by creating more liberty, more fraternity, more justice than the world had ever seen. Now, while mankind laboured at this task of spiritualization, inferior powers--I was going to say infernal powers--plotted an inverse experience for mankind. What would happen if the mechanical forces, which science had brought to a state of readiness for the service of man, should themselves take possession of man in order to make his nature material as their own? What kind of a world would it be if this mechanism should seize the human race entire, and if the peoples, instead of raising themselves to a richer and more harmonious diversity, as *persons* may do, were to fall into the uniformity of *things*? What kind of a society would that be which should mechanically obey a word of command mechanically transmitted; which should rule its science and its conscience in accordance therewith; and which should lose, along with the sense of justice, the power to discern between truth and falsehood? What would mankind be when brute force should hold the place of moral force? What new barbarism, this time final, would arise from these conditions to stifle feeling, ideas, and the whole civilization of which the old barbarism contained the germ? What would happen, in short, if the moral effort of humanity should turn in its tracks at the moment of attaining its goal, and if some diabolical contrivance should cause it to produce the mechanization of spirit instead of the spiritualization of matter? There was a people predestined to try the experiment. Prussia had been militarized by her kings; Germany had been militarized by Prussia; a powerful nation was on the spot marching forward in mechanical order. Administration and military mechanism were only waiting to make alliance with industrial mechanism. The combination once made, a formidable machine would come into existence. A touch upon the starting-gear and the other nations would be dragged in the wake of Germany, subjects to the same movement, prisoners of the same mechanism. Such would be the meaning of the war on the day when Germany should decide upon its declaration.

She decided, he will continue, but the result was very different from what had been predicted. For the moral forces, which were to submit to the forces of matter by their side, suddenly revealed themselves as creators of material force. A simple idea, the heroic conception which a small people had formed of its honour, enabled it to make head against a powerful empire. At the cry of outraged justice we saw, moreover, in a nation which till then had trusted in its fleet, one million, two millions of soldiers suddenly rise from the earth. A yet greater miracle: in a nation thought to be mortally divided against itself all became brothers in the space of a day. From that moment the issue of the conflict was not open to doubt. On the one side, there was force spread out on the surface; on the other, there was force in the depths. On one side, mechanism, the manufactured article which cannot repair its own injuries; on the other, life, the power of creation which makes and remakes itself at every instant. On one side, that which uses itself up; on the other, that which does not use itself up.

Indeed, our philosopher will conclude, the machine did use itself up. For a long time it resisted; then it bent; then it broke. Alas! it had crushed under it a multitude of our children; and over the fate of this young life, which was so naturally and purely heroic, our tears will continue to fall. An implacable law decrees that spirit must encounter the resistance of matter, that life cannot advance without bruising that which lives, and that great moral results are purchased by much blood and by many tears. But this time the sacrifice was to be rich in fruit as it had been rich in beauty. That the powers of death might be matched against life in one supreme combat, destiny had gathered them all at a single point. And behold how death was conquered; how humanity was saved by material suffering from the moral downfall which would have been its end; while the peoples, joyful in their desolation, raised on high the song of deliverance from the depths of ruin and of grief!

THE FORCE WHICH WASTES AND THAT WHICH DOES NOT WASTE

THE issue of the struggle is not doubtful. Germany will succumb. Material force and moral force, all which is sustaining her, will end by failing her, because she is living on provision she has accumulated, is spending it, and has no way of renewing it.

Of her material resources all is known. She has money, but her credit is falling, and one does not see where she is to borrow. She needs nitrates for her explosives, fuel for her motors, bread for her sixty-five million inhabitants, for all of which she has made provision; but the day will come when her granaries will be empty and her tanks dry. How will she refill them? War, as she practises it, makes frightful havoc of her warriors. Yet here again replenishment is impossible, no aid will come from without, because an enterprise launched with the object of imposing German rule, German "culture," German products, only interests and ever will only interest what is already German. Such is the situation of Germany confronted by a France who is keeping her credit intact and her ports open, who is procuring herself victual and munitions as she pleases, who reinforces her armies with all that her allies bring to her support, and who can count on the ever more active sympathy of the civilized world because her cause is that of humanity itself.

Still this is only material force, the force which is seen. What can we say of moral force, the force which is not seen, which yet matters most since it can in a certain degree make good what is lacking of the other, and without which the other is worthless?

The moral energy of nations, as of individuals, is only sustained by an ideal higher than themselves, and stronger than themselves, to which they cling firmly when they feel their courage waver. Where is the ideal of the Germany of to-day?

The time when her philosophers proclaimed the inviolability of right, the eminent dignity of the person, the duty of mutual respect among nations, is no more. Germany, militarized by Prussia, has cast aside those noble ideas, ideas she received for the most part from the France of the eighteenth century and of the Revolution. She has made for herself a new soul, or rather she has meekly accepted the soul Bismarck has given her. To him has been attributed the famous maxim "Might is right." But in truth Bismarck never pronounced it, for he had well guarded himself against a distinction of right from might. Right was simply in his view what is willed by the strongest, what is consigned by the conqueror in the law he imposes on the conquered. In that is summed up his whole morality. Germany to-day knows no other. She, too, worships brute force. And because she believes herself the strongest, she is altogether absorbed in self-adoration. Her energy comes from her pride. Her moral force is only the confidence which her material force inspires in her. And this means that in this respect she is living on reserves without means of replenishment. Even before England had commenced to blockade her coasts she had blockaded herself morally, in isolating herself from every ideal capable of giving her new life.

So she will see her forces waste and her courage at the same time. But the energy of our soldiers is drawn from something which does not waste, from an ideal of justice and freedom. Time has no hold on us. To the force which feeds only on its own brutality we are opposing that which seeks outside and above itself a principle of life and renovation. Whilst the one is gradually spending itself, the other is continually remaking itself. The one is already wavering, the other abides unshaken. Have no fear, our force will slay theirs.

www.bookjungle.com email: sales@bookjungle.com fax: 630-214-0564 mail: Book Jungle PO Box 2226 Champaign, IL 61825

The Codes Of Hammurabi And Moses
W. W. Davies

QTY

The discovery of the Hammurabi Code is one of the greatest achievements of archaeology, and is of paramount interest, not only to the student of the Bible, but also to all those interested in ancient history...

Religion   ISBN: *1-59462-338-4*   Pages:132   MSRP *$12.95*

The Theory of Moral Sentiments
Adam Smith

QTY

This work from 1749. contains original theories of conscience amd moral judgment and it is the foundation for systemof morals.

Philosophy   ISBN: *1-59462-777-0*   Pages:536   MSRP *$19.95*

Jessica's First Prayer
Hesba Stretton

QTY

In a screened and secluded corner of one of the many railway-bridges which span the streets of London there could be seen a few years ago, from five o'clock every morning until half past eight, a tidily set-out coffee-stall, consisting of a trestle and board, upon which stood two large tin cans, with a small fire of charcoal burning under each so as to keep the coffee boiling during the early hours of the morning when the work-people were thronging into the city on their way to their daily toil...

Childrens   ISBN: *1-59462-373-2*   Pages:84   MSRP *$9.95*

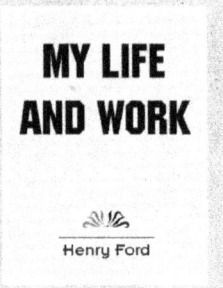

My Life and Work
Henry Ford

QTY

Henry Ford revolutionized the world with his implementation of mass production for the Model T automobile. Gain valuable business insight into his life and work with his own auto-biography... "We have only started on our development of our country we have not as yet, with all our talk of wonderful progress, done more than scratch the surface. The progress has been wonderful enough but..."

Biographies/   ISBN: *1-59462-198-5*   Pages:300   MSRP *$21.95* www.bookjungle.com *email: sales@bookjungle.com fax: 630-214-0564 mail: Book Jungle PO Box 2226 Champaign, IL 61825*

The Art of Cross-Examination
Francis Wellman

I presume it is the experience of every author, after his first book is published upon an important subject, to be almost overwhelmed with a wealth of ideas and illustrations which could readily have been included in his book, and which to his own mind, at least, seem to make a second edition inevitable. Such certainly was the case with me; and when the first edition had reached its sixth impression in five months, I rejoiced to learn that it seemed to my publishers that the book had met with a sufficiently favorable reception to justify a second and considerably enlarged edition. ...

QTY

Reference   ISBN: *1-59462-647-2*

Pages:412
MSRP $19.95

On the Duty of Civil Disobedience
Henry David Thoreau

Thoreau wrote his famous essay, On the Duty of Civil Disobedience, as a protest against an unjust but popular war and the immoral but popular institution of slave-owning. He did more than write—he declined to pay his taxes, and was hauled off to gaol in consequence. Who can say how much this refusal of his hastened the end of the war and of slavery?

QTY

Law   ISBN: *1-59462-747-9*

Pages:48
MSRP $7.45

Dream Psychology Psychoanalysis for Beginners
Sigmund Freud

Sigmund Freud, born Sigismund Schlomo Freud (May 6, 1856 - September 23, 1939), was a Jewish-Austrian neurologist and psychiatrist who co-founded the psychoanalytic school of psychology. Freud is best known for his theories of the unconscious mind, especially involving the mechanism of repression; his redefinition of sexual desire as mobile and directed towards a wide variety of objects; and his therapeutic techniques, especially his understanding of transference in the therapeutic relationship and the presumed value of dreams as sources of insight into unconscious desires.

QTY

Psychology   ISBN: *1-59462-905-6*

Pages:196
MSRP $15.45

The Miracle of Right Thought
Orison Swett Marden

Believe with all of your heart that you will do what you were made to do. When the mind has once formed the habit of holding cheerful, happy, prosperous pictures, it will not be easy to form the opposite habit. It does not matter how improbable or how far away this realization may see, or how dark the prospects may be, if we visualize them as best we can, as vividly as possible, hold tenaciously to them and vigorously struggle to attain them, they will gradually become actualized, realized in the life. But a desire, a longing without endeavor, a yearning abandoned or held indifferently will vanish without realization.

QTY

Self Help   ISBN: *1-59462-644-8*

Pages:360
MSRP $25.45

www.bookjungle.com email: sales@bookjungle.com fax: 630-214-0564 mail: Book Jungle PO Box 2226 Champaign, IL 61825

QTY

| | **The Rosicrucian Cosmo-Conception Mystic Christianity** by *Max Heindel* — ISBN: *1-59462-188-8* **$38.95** |
| The Rosicrucian Cosmo-conception is not dogmatic, neither does it appeal to any other authority than the reason of the student. It is: not controversial, but is: sent forth in the, hope that it may help to clear... — New Age/Religion Pages 646 |

☐ **Abandonment To Divine Providence** by *Jean-Pierre de Caussade* — ISBN: *1-59462-228-0* **$25.95**
"The Rev. Jean Pierre de Caussade was one of the most remarkable spiritual writers of the Society of Jesus in France in the 18th Century. His death took place at Toulouse in 1751. His works have gone through many editions and have been republished... — Inspirational/Religion Pages 400

☐ **Mental Chemistry** by *Charles Haanel* — ISBN: *1-59462-192-6* **$23.95**
Mental Chemistry allows the change of material conditions by combining and appropriately utilizing the power of the mind. Much like applied chemistry creates something new and unique out of careful combinations of chemicals the mastery of mental chemistry... — New Age Pages 354

☐ **The Letters of Robert Browning and Elizabeth Barret Barrett 1845-1846 vol II** — ISBN: *1-59462-193-4* **$35.95**
by *Robert Browning* and *Elizabeth Barrett* — Biographies Pages 596

☐ **Gleanings In Genesis (volume I)** by *Arthur W. Pink* — ISBN: *1-59462-130-6* **$27.45**
Appropriately has Genesis been termed "the seed plot of the Bible" for in it we have, in germ form, almost all of the great doctrines which are afterwards fully developed in the books of Scripture which follow... — Religion/Inspirational Pages 420

☐ **The Master Key** by *L. W. de Laurence* — ISBN: *1-59462-001-6* **$30.95**
In no branch of human knowledge has there been a more lively increase of the spirit of research during the past few years than in the study of Psychology, Concentration and Mental Discipline. The requests for authentic lessons in Thought Control, Mental Discipline and... — New Age/Business Pages 422

☐ **The Lesser Key Of Solomon Goetia** by *L. W. de Laurence* — ISBN: *1-59462-092-X* **$9.95**
This translation of the first book of the "Lemegton" which is now for the first time made accessible to students of Talismanic Magic was done, after careful collation and edition, from numerous Ancient Manuscripts in Hebrew, Latin, and French... — New Age/Occult Pages 92

☐ **Rubaiyat Of Omar Khayyam** by *Edward Fitzgerald* — ISBN: *1-59462-332-5* **$13.95**
Edward Fitzgerald, whom the world has already learned, in spite of his own efforts to remain within the shadow of anonymity, to look upon as one of the rarest poets of the century, was born at Bredfield, in Suffolk, on the 31st of March, 1809. He was the third son of John Purcell... — Music Pages 172

☐ **Ancient Law** by *Henry Maine* — ISBN: *1-59462-128-4* **$29.95**
The chief object of the following pages is to indicate some of the earliest ideas of mankind, as they are reflected in Ancient Law, and to point out the relation of those ideas to modern thought. — Religiom/History Pages 452

☐ **Far-Away Stories** by *William J. Locke* — ISBN: *1-59462-129-2* **$19.45**
"Good wine needs no bush, but a collection of mixed vintages does. And this book is just such a collection. Some of the stories I do not want to remain buried for ever in the museum files of dead magazine-numbers an author's not unpardonable vanity..." — Fiction Pages 272

☐ **Life of David Crockett** by *David Crockett* — ISBN: *1-59462-250-7* **$27.45**
"Colonel David Crockett was one of the most remarkable men of the times in which he lived. Born in humble life, but gifted with a strong will, an indomitable courage, and unremitting perseverance... — Biographies/New Age Pages 424

☐ **Lip-Reading** by *Edward Nitchie* — ISBN: *1-59462-206-X* **$25.95**
Edward B. Nitchie, founder of the New York School for the Hard of Hearing, now the Nitchie School of Lip-Reading, Inc, wrote "LIP-READING Principles and Practice". The development and perfecting of this meritorious work on lip-reading was an undertaking... — How-to Pages 400

☐ **A Handbook of Suggestive Therapeutics, Applied Hypnotism, Psychic Science** — ISBN: *1-59462-214-0* **$24.95**
by *Henry Munro* — Health/New Age/Health/Self-help Pages 376

☐ **A Doll's House: and Two Other Plays** by *Henrik Ibsen* — ISBN: *1-59462-112-8* **$19.95**
Henrik Ibsen created this classic when in revolutionary 1848 Rome. Introducing some striking concepts in playwriting for the realist genre, this play has been studied the world over. — Fiction/Classics/Plays 308

☐ **The Light of Asia** by *sir Edwin Arnold* — ISBN: *1-59462-204-3* **$13.95**
In this poetic masterpiece, Edwin Arnold describes the life and teachings of Buddha. The man who was to become known as Buddha to the world was born as Prince Gautama of India but he rejected the worldly riches and abandoned the reigns of power when... — Religion/History/Biographies Pages 170

☐ **The Complete Works of Guy de Maupassant** by *Guy de Maupassant* — ISBN: *1-59462-157-8* **$16.95**
"For days and days, nights and nights, I had dreamed of that first kiss which was to consecrate our engagement, and I knew not on what spot I should put my lips..." — Fiction/Classics Pages 240

☐ **The Art of Cross-Examination** by *Francis L. Wellman* — ISBN: *1-59462-309-0* **$26.95**
Written by a renowned trial lawyer, Wellman imparts his experience and uses case studies to explain how to use psychology to extract desired information through questioning. — How-to/Science/Reference Pages 408

☐ **Answered or Unanswered?** by *Louisa Vaughan* — ISBN: *1-59462-248-5* **$10.95**
Miracles of Faith in China — Religion Pages 112

☐ **The Edinburgh Lectures on Mental Science (1909)** by *Thomas* — ISBN: *1-59462-008-3* **$11.95**
This book contains the substance of a course of lectures recently given by the writer in the Queen Street Hall, Edinburgh. Its purpose is to indicate the Natural Principles governing the relation between Mental Action and Material Conditions... — New Age/Psychology Pages 148

☐ **Ayesha** by *H. Rider Haggard* — ISBN: *1-59462-301-5* **$24.95**
Verily and indeed it is the unexpected that happens! Probably if there was one person upon the earth from whom the Editor of this, and of a certain previous history, did not expect to hear again... — Classics Pages 380

☐ **Ayala's Angel** by *Anthony Trollope* — ISBN: *1-59462-352-X* **$29.95**
The two girls were both pretty, but Lucy who was twenty-one who supposed to be simple and comparatively unattractive, whereas Ayala was credited, as her Bombwhat romantic name might show, with poetic charm and a taste for romance. Ayala when her father died was nineteen... — Fiction Pages 484

☐ **The American Commonwealth** by *James Bryce* — ISBN: *1-59462-286-8* **$34.45**
An interpretation of American democratic political theory. It examines political mechanics and society from the perspective of Scotsman James Bryce — Politics Pages 572

☐ **Stories of the Pilgrims** by *Margaret P. Pumphrey* — ISBN: *1-59462-116-0* **$17.95**
This book explores pilgrims religious oppression in England as well as their escape to Holland and eventual crossing to America on the Mayflower, and their early days in New England... — History Pages 268

www.bookjungle.com email: sales@bookjungle.com fax: 630-214-0564 mail: Book Jungle PO Box 2226 Champaign, IL 61825

Title	ISBN	Price	QTY
The Fasting Cure by *Sinclair Upton* — In the Cosmopolitan Magazine for May, 1910, and in the Contemporary Review (London) for April, 1910, I published an article dealing with my experiences in fasting. I have written a great many magazine articles, but never one which attracted so much attention... *New Age/Self Help/Health Pages 164*	1-59462-222-1	$13.95	
Hebrew Astrology by *Sepharial* — In these days of advanced thinking it is a matter of common observation that we have left many of the old landmarks behind and that we are now pressing forward to greater heights and to a wider horizon than that which represented the mind-content of our progenitors... *Astrology Pages 144*	1-59462-308-2	$13.45	
Thought Vibration or The Law of Attraction in the Thought World by *William Walker Atkinson* — *Psychology/Religion Pages 144*	1-59462-127-6	$12.95	
Optimism by *Helen Keller* — Helen Keller was blind, deaf, and mute since 19 months old, yet famously learned how to overcome these handicaps, communicate with the world, and spread her lectures promoting optimism. An inspiring read for everyone... *Biographies/Inspirational Pages 84*	1-59462-108-X	$15.95	
Sara Crewe by *Frances Burnett* — In the first place, Miss Minchin lived in London. Her home was a large, dull, tall one, in a large, dull square, where all the houses were alike, and all the sparrows were alike, and where all the door-knockers made the same heavy sound... *Childrens/Classic Pages 88*	1-59462-360-0	$9.45	
The Autobiography of Benjamin Franklin by *Benjamin Franklin* — The Autobiography of Benjamin Franklin has probably been more extensively read than any other American historical work, and no other book of its kind has had such ups and downs of fortune. Franklin lived for many years in England, where he was agent... *Biographies/History Pages 332*	1-59462-135-7	$24.95	

Name	
Email	
Telephone	
Address	
City, State ZIP	

☐ Credit Card   ☐ Check / Money Order

Credit Card Number	
Expiration Date	
Signature	

Please Mail to: Book Jungle
PO Box 2226
Champaign, IL 61825
or Fax to: 630-214-0564

ORDERING INFORMATION

web: www.bookjungle.com
email: sales@bookjungle.com
fax: 630-214-0564
mail: Book Jungle PO Box 2226 Champaign, IL 61825
or PayPal to sales@bookjungle.com

Please contact us for bulk discounts

DIRECT-ORDER TERMS

20% Discount if You Order Two or More Books
Free Domestic Shipping!
Accepted: Master Card, Visa, Discover, American Express

www.ingramcontent.com/pod-product-compliance
Lightning Source LLC
Chambersburg PA
CBHW081350040426
42450CB00015B/3384